EXPLORING

URANUS

By Cody Keiser

KidHaven
PUBLISHING

Published in 2018 by
KidHaven Publishing, an Imprint of Greenhaven Publishing, LLC
353 3rd Avenue
Suite 255
New York, NY 10010

Designer: Deanna Paternostro
Editor: Vanessa Oswald

Photo credits: Cover, back cover, pp. 7, 19 (main) Vadim Sadovski/Shutterstock.com; pp. 4–5 ANDRZEJ WOJCICKI/SCIENCE PHOTO LIBRARY/Getty Images; p. 9 (main) shooarts/ Shutterstock.com; p. 9 (inset) Tfr000/Wikimedia Commons; p. 11 Catmando/Shutterstock.com; p. 13 SkyPics Studio/Shutterstock.com; pp. 15, 19 (inset) Time Life Pictures/Contributor/The LIFE Picture Collection/Getty Images; p. 17 Jcpag2012/Wikimedia Commons; p. 21 Orange-kun/Wikimedia Commons.

Cataloging-in-Publication Data

Names: Keiser, Cody.
Title: Exploring Uranus / Cody Keiser.
Description: New York : KidHaven Publishing, 2018. | Series: Journey through our solar system | Includes index.
Identifiers: ISBN 9781534522893 (pbk.) | 9781534522817 (library bound) | ISBN 9781534522534 (6 pack) | ISBN 9781534522640 (ebook)
Subjects: LCSH: Uranus (Planet)–Juvenile literature.
Classification: LCC QB681.K395 2018 | DDC 523.47–dc23
Printed in the United States of America

CPSIA compliance information: Batch #BS17KL: For further information contact Greenhaven Publishing LLC, New York, New York at 1-844-317-7404.

Please visit our website, www.greenhavenpublishing.com. For a free color catalog of all our high-quality books, call toll free 1-844-317-7404 or fax 1-844-317-7405.

CONTENTS

ICE PLANET

Uranus is the third-largest planet and the seventh planet from the sun in the **solar system**.

Neptune

Uranus

Saturn

Jupiter

It's about four times wider than Earth. Being so far away from the sun makes it very cold and icy.

Uranus most likely formed close to the sun and moved away from it about 4 billion years ago.

Mars

Earth

Venus

Mercury

sun

MOVING AND SPINNING

Like the other planets, Uranus **orbits** the sun. It takes Uranus 84 Earth years to orbit the sun once. It orbits slowly, but it spins much faster. It only takes 17 hours to spin around once!

Uranus

sun

The planets, including Uranus, rotate, or spin around an axis, which is an imaginary line through the middle of a planet.

Uranus doesn't spin like most of the other planets. It spins in the opposite direction, which is called a retrograde rotation. Uranus is also different because it spins on its side!

The only other planet that has a retrograde rotation is Venus.

Earth's rotation

Uranus's rotation

sun

Uranus

IT'S COLD!

Uranus has the coldest weather in the solar system. Icy clouds made up of the gases hydrogen, helium, and **surround** the planet. Methane makes Uranus look blue-green.

Frozen methane gives Uranus a cool blue color!

Scientists think a giant ocean made up of water, **ammonia**, and methane ices can be found beneath the clouds of Uranus. They also think there's a rocky core at the center of the planet.

hydrogen, helium,
and methane gases

water, ammonia,
and methane ices

rocky core

The core of Uranus is
9,000 degrees Fahrenheit
(4,982 degrees Celsius).

RINGS AND MOONS

Thirteen rings surround Uranus. It has a set of inner rings and outer rings. The inner group has nine rings, and the outer group has four rings.

Uranus's rings are made of large chunks of rock.

rings

Uranus has 27 small moons. All the planet's inner moons are made of water, ice, and rock. Some scientists think the outer moons are **captured asteroids.**

moon

Uranus

moons

moons

Uranus's moons were
first discovered in 1787.

STUDYING URANUS

The *Voyager 2* **probe** is the only spaceship that's visited Uranus so far. It launched in 1977 and traveled more than 1.8 billion miles (3 billion km). It took nine years to reach Uranus. The probe discovered many of the planet's rings and moons in six hours.

A spaceship couldn't land on Uranus because there isn't solid ground!

Uranus

Voyager 2
probe

Future **missions** to visit Uranus are planned for the late 2020s. Scientists can't wait to find out more about this cool planet!

If Uranus was the size
of a softball, Earth would
be about as big as a nickel.

Uranus

Earth

GLOSSARY

ammonia: A colorless gas with a strong smell.

captured asteroid: A large space rock caught in a planet's orbit.

mission: A definite task involving space.

orbit: To travel in a circle or oval around something.

probe: A vehicle that sends information about an object in space back to Earth.

solar system: The sun and all the space objects that orbit it, including planets and their moons.

surround: To be on every side of something.

FOR MORE INFORMATION

Websites

NASA Space Place: All About Uranus
spaceplace.nasa.gov/all-about-uranus/en/
NASA's website gives visitors a closer look
at Uranus.

National Geographic Kids: Mission to Uranus
kids.nationalgeographic.com/explore/space/
mission-to-uranus/#uranus-planet.jpg
This website presents fun facts about Uranus.

Books

Adamson, Thomas K. *The Secrets of Uranus*. North
Mankato, MN: Capstone Press, 2016.

Bloom, J.P. *Uranus*. Minneapolis, MN: Abdo Kids, 2015.

Glaser, Chaya. *Uranus: Cold and Blue*. New York, NY:
Bearport Publishing, 2015.

INDEX